RUGBY
Gave Me Hope

Credits
Written by : Rick Kirkland
Illustrations by: Sha-Nee Williams
Creative Editing by : Ashley Watkins
Inspired by: YOU

I am HoshiToshi. Call me Hoshi!

My name is native for 'enjoy life, spread love and inspire'. I like all three meanings of my name, equally. They make me feel as unique as my name sounds; Ha-she – Ta-she! I am pleased that for most of my life, I have lived out those meanings, too. In many ways, but particularly in one special way, you'll learn just how I've enjoyed life, spread love and inspired others along the way!

My life began in one of the historic cities in the state of New Jersey – Paterson. Paterson, New Jersey's manufacturing center for producing silk, is nicknamed Silk City. It is also home of the Great Falls of the Passaic River. I happen to be the oldest of three siblings raised there by my single-parent mother. We lived together in the Christopher Columbus Projects. Even as a child, I was aware that we lived in a low-income, government house. In our neighborhood, people weren't expected to dream as much or as big as others. I, however, had lots of dreams!

At the age of six, my biggest dream was becoming a professional football player. I remember being one of the youngest players among my cousin and other athletic friends who loved playing football, too. They were excellent players and very inspiring to me. Quite often, I'd try to show off my 'Pick up and Tackle', 'Tag' and 'Hold Hit' skills to prove to them that I could play just as well. Although I fell short many times, they motivated me to practice playing the game with passion and drive. And I did!

In my mind, playing professional football was going to make me rich! Yes, rich! I was going to make lots and lots of money, all while playing a game I loved. Then, I would use that money to help myself and family to move out of the projects, for good. Others, like me, would learn of my story and be inspired to do the same for themselves and their families. At last, everyone in the projects could leave them behind, hence no more need for them. It was supposed to be that simple.

My biggest inspiration for a better life was at home. I'd often watch my mother work very hard to give my siblings and me a more than comfortable life. She was incredibly strong and determined to achieve success at being a single mother. And she ROCKED it! I wanted to be everything that she was and more, so I put all my effort into playing football. I consistently worked hard at being good enough to go Pro!

Playing sports became more than just football.
I noticed that I was becoming more self-disciplined.
I had to be present for practice and games and play my
hardest, even if my energy level was not the highest
on game day. Soon, every single playing experience
taught me more about myself, what I had inside of me
and what I could achieve as long as I put in the work.
Football became a new way for me to express myself –
to live out the full meanings of HoshiToshi!

HOSHI TOSHI

Nickname: Unstoppable
Age: 12
Grade: 8th
Pos: WR

Sometimes, I use to go to a park area along the famous Hudson River and just daydream. I mostly pictured the day when I would have finally gone Pro. I would be able to start making a difference in the world, right away. One day, as I watched the early evening change to night, the lights in the skyline of New York City flickered on, one by one, like I'd never noticed before. In that moment, I imagined myself as one of those lights, finally coming on for Paterson through football, and shining the way for others to see their way out of the projects. That feeling I had was new and most memorable!

Of course, the skyline also reminded me of the Big Apple where great movies are made and talented celebrities live their best lives. That night, I fell asleep with the thought of one day being among them and belonging, too.

Following my dream, I was eight years old in the 4th grade when I officially became a part of a football team. At first, I was not playing much, but then a team member left the game due to his poor grades in school, opening up the opportunity for me to get on the field and in the game.

Remember, up to this moment, the plan was simple; Earn a spot to play, give it my best shot, get noticed as a star and go Pro. I was beside myself with joy to have entered the first stage of the plan! However, as this chance was finally here, I had a big problem. At game time, I would show up super nervous, holding back from playing as hard as I knew I could. It would take me some time to finally break through that season in my life. Luckily, as things turned around, I became more and more confident on the field, making key plays to help my team to victory. Before too long, I, HoshiToshi, was making a name for myself as a key player in football. YES! I'd stuck to it and was a star football player in the making! In my mind, playing professional football was only a matter of time.

Years later, I would go on to play American football in college. I practiced hard and played with a lot of passion, still aiming to go Pro. By now, my heart was set on becoming an NFL player. My whole college experience was very uplifting. I grew a lot as an athlete in college and increased my knowledge about other forms of sports, including a game called Rugby.

Rugby started in 1823 and is rated second in the world of sports, next to Soccer which is number one. Before now, I'd honestly never heard about the game. It was introduced to me by a friend who, after seeing me play football at school, thought that I had the discipline and passion for sports that would make me a great player of Rugby, too.

Following my desire to attain greatness, I accepted my friend's invitation to check out a game of Rugby. I was fascinated by his idea of me playing and possibly making the Olympic Rugby team. However, as I observed the game, I knew right away that Rugby was not for me. I mean, unlike football, the players had no equipment, plus their shorts made me think of very uncomfortable fitting clothes. That was enough for me to choose not to play Rugby at the time, but instead focus on football and my dream of making it to the NFL.

Well, I'd finished college and, unfortunately, had not achieved my NFL dream. Sure, I was disappointed about having to live a regular life instead of the famous lifestyle I had imagined. However, with a name like mine, I decided to enjoy life and shine like a star to inspire others in other ways. And, I could not think of a better way to do this than to work with children. I successfully gained employment working with special children who were living with Autism spectrum disorder. Immediately, I was in love with the whole experience!

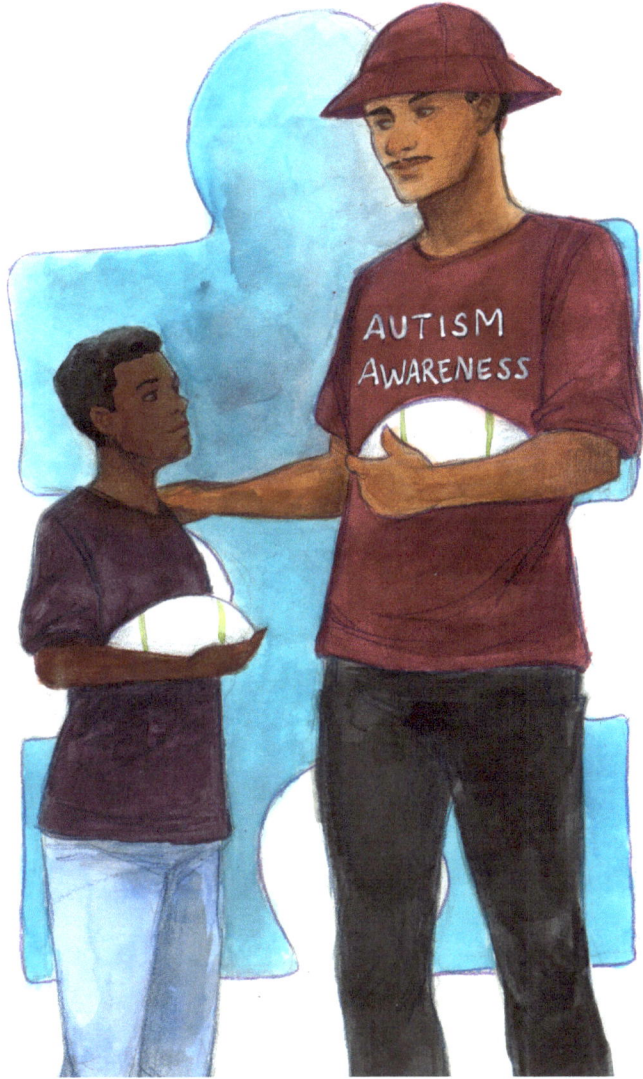

Autism spectrum disorder is a challenging condition that affects the way that some children grow. They may have a harder time making friends, expressing themselves to the world and/or controlling their daily behaviors. My job was to be very patient and creative in working with these children to help them function as best as possible in the world. Of course, I used sports, music, and positive energy to successfully engage them. You got it! Here I was, applying my athletic skills in a work environment, and totally loving it! I was reminding myself of my true passion for sports.

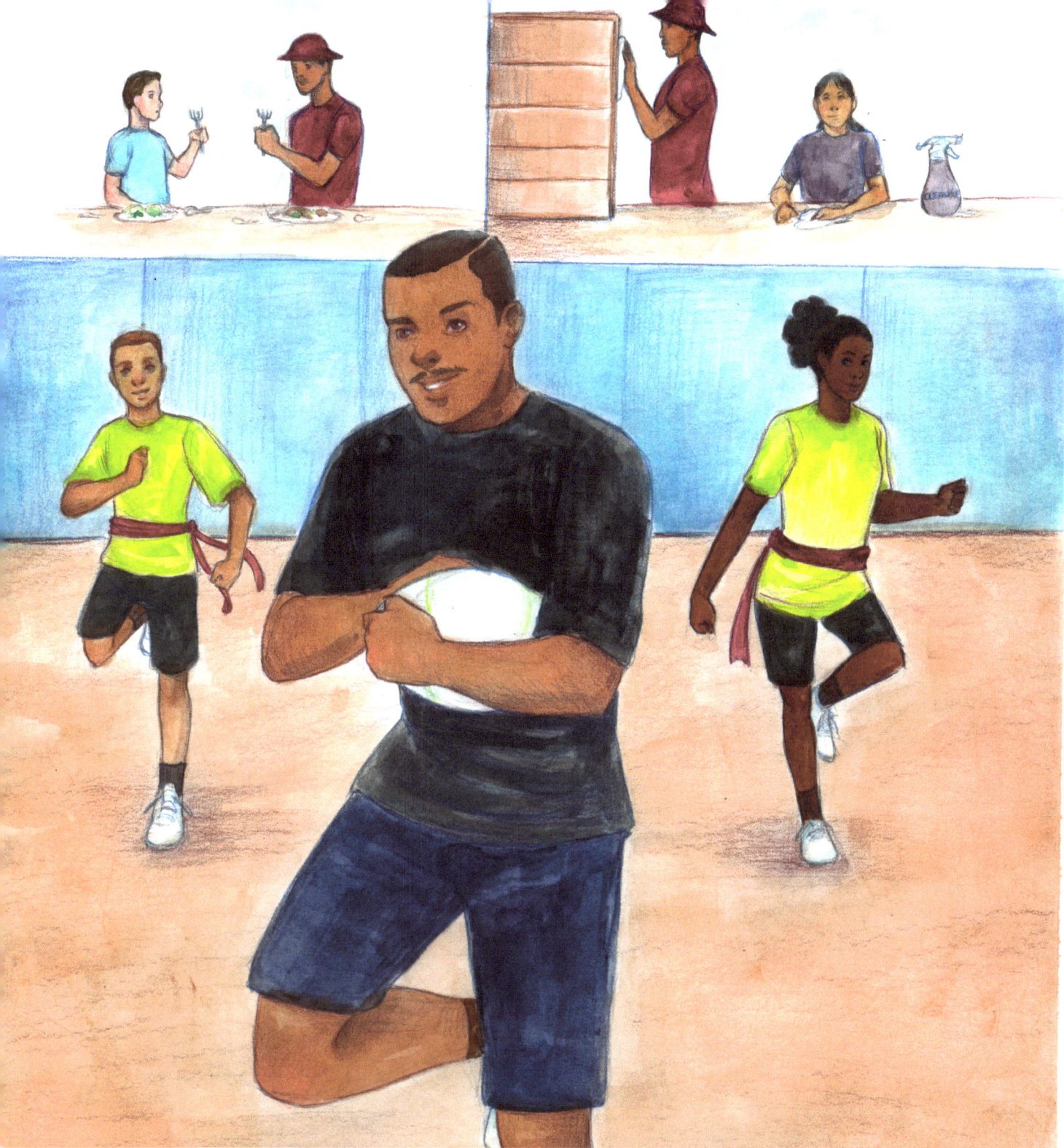

So, while I truly enjoyed my job working with special children, and welcomed being promoted to Supervisor, I longed to play football! Sure, I was pleased that I still had a lot of passion and drive inside of me to achieve whatever I put my mind toward. Teaching children was extremely rewarding for me. However, something was missing from my life! I finally gave in to the fact that I had to play sports again – my truest passion and drive!

That's when I reached out to my old friend about giving the game of Rugby a serious trial. He was excited and I was willing, so we made plans for me to play for a local club in New Haven, Connecticut, just a little over two hours away from home. Once again, I was on a path I was convinced was designed for me!

A few things about Rugby were similar to football – only a few. Like football, the team was very close and willing to give support to each other. The game also required a lot of discipline from me. I had to go to training early in order to learn the rules of the game and improve my playing skills. However, Rugby was not football – my first love! I struggled to fall in love with the game in the same way I did with football. I wanted to give up several times, but the thought of becoming a star and inspiring Paterson and the world, helped me stick to it.

The rules of playing Rugby seemed to be quite different from all other sports I had ever played. All the passes were backward and it was strange to me that, unlike American football, once the player got into the area to score points, the Try Zone, he would have to touch the ball on the ground with full control. This would count as a valid score. Unlike football, Rugby continued for the playing time, unless a team scored or there was a call for penalty. I found it confusing and challenging at first.

① Scoring A Try

② Backward Passes

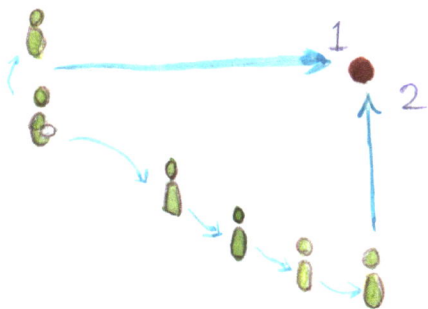

1

2

Never-the-less, I quickly learned Rugby,
with its rules and strange practices. I was able to apply
skills I had learned from playing basketball, American
football and even running track and field, to master the
game! I truly enjoyed sporting again, being a part of
a team and working together to meet our goals. I was
back where I belonged.

Before too long, Hoshi Toshi and my rugby
team were a household name. The Rugby community
loved us and celebrated our successes in playing quality
Rugby. At last, I was seeing the evidence of the full
meaning of my name – enjoying life, spreading love and
inspiring others.

At the peak of my play, I was invited to play for an Olympic Development Academy. There, I received high-level coaching and practiced among some very experienced Rugby players. Yes! That was the beginning of a new day for me. Soon, I was invited to move to New York City, the city where great movies and celebrities are made. I had achieved my goal of playing at an even higher level in Rugby.

I reflected on the days that I used to daydream about this goal. I had pictured myself in that moment a thousand or more times over. To finally achieve it was amazing and it gave me a new sense of wanting – even needing – to stick to the vision of my complete dream. I was sure to be successful. I never felt closer to seeing it all happen!

New York City was exciting! There, I met Rugby players from all over the world including faraway places like Europe, Australia, and New Zealand. I learned more about the game and became even more successful at playing. Eventually, I played against other players who were members of the official USA Rugby team. That's right! I was getting closer to my ideal dream. That experience was self-inspiring!

But I had not quite abandoned the life of working with children altogether. In the daytime, I had the opportunity to work with children from communities that were a lot like Paterson. I found it super interesting that when I met these children, my Passion to inspire others matched their needs for learning life skills. I was in my mid 20s by this time. These children were learning Rugby during some of their most impressionable years, ages of 7-12 years. I was honored to be a part of their journey. Talk about spreading love!

I witnessed at-risk children who were less likely to successfully move into adulthood, become inspired by my sportsmanship as well as sports. Playing Rugby, they believed in themselves and felt empowered to do and be more than what was expected of them in their various communities. Each child I met reminded me of someone I knew – ME! Altogether, they inspired me to never give up my own dream of being among the greats in sports.

Over the years, I saw Rugby influence whole communities to change from stress to peace; from drama and trauma to harmony, and from anxiety and bullying to true teamwork and partnership. Wow! Children learned positive competition and finding solutions to their problems among themselves – skills that were necessary for leading them into better adulthood lives, hence better citizens of life. I was proud to witness these experiences from one community to the next.

Thankfully, I've lived out what I imagined for myself while growing up in the projects of Paterson. Rugby inspired me and allowed me to be an inspiration to others as well. Although, I did not become rich from the sport of Rugby , I've been fortunate to travel the world as an athlete, visiting countries in the Midwest, West Coast, Singapore, Ireland, Portugal, France, Tobago, and Barbados. Today, Rugby is currently one of the fastest growing sports in the United States.

Hopefully, my story has interested you in accessing some opportunities to learn about and get involved in Rugby – the game that changed my life! Simply get involved in your local youth clubs, high school or college teams, local men and women Rugby union and league clubs. Seek out and explore scholarship possibilities and work hard at playing professional Rugby at league or major league levels, including for the USA team. You have what it takes – just like me!

Life is spectacular! I've learned that spreading love and inspiring others has a special reward. It's simply the interesting way that life works. When you give, you'll receive. For giving of my talent and skills in sports to the children, supporters, family and friends as well as the world, life has shown me a unique appreciation in self-satisfaction.

I encourage everyone who reads this book to give of yourself to someone else, at least once daily. You might need to practice and remain consistent, especially if giving does not come naturally to you. Remember how I mastered Rugby? In the same way, you can do anything! When you give, you'll feel great about doing something for someone else other than yourself. After that, when it comes to helping, sharing love and being an inspiration to others, no doubt, you'll be a PRO!

www.ingramcontent.com/pod-product-compliance
Lightning Source LLC
Chambersburg PA
CBHW042010090426
42811CB00015B/1607